UP CLOSE
& PERSONAL

UP CLOSE
& PERSONAL

Stories of Courage in the Midst of Devastation

COLIN ALEXANDER

authorHOUSE®

AuthorHouse™
1663 Liberty Drive
Bloomington, IN 47403
www.authorhouse.com
Phone: 1-800-839-8640

Published by AuthorHouse   03/30/2012

ISBN: 978-1-4685-7558-3 (sc)

Library of Congress Control Number: 2012905934

Any people depicted in stock imagery provided by Thinkstock are models, and such images are being used for illustrative purposes only.
Certain stock imagery © Thinkstock.

This book is printed on acid-free paper.

"Love, passion, obsession, all those things you told me to wait for, well, they've arrived."

This quote, taken from the movie, "Meet Joe Black," describes how I feel about my life. I am indebted to my wonderful wife, Linda, and my two beautiful children, Alex and Ally, for inspiring me to do what brings me passion, for giving me room for my obsession, and for providing me the love to make it happen.

Thank you guys!

Colin

Contents

Introduction

When I was a young kid, perhaps 10 or 11, I had what most would consider a strange quirk: I liked hanging out in cemeteries. The particular cemetery I frequented most was old, antiquated you might say, and adorned with historical character, thus it always made for an enjoyable time. As this habit was a little out of the norm for a boy my age, many of my friends considered me a bit weird and, thus, would not accompany me to the cemetery. Though I was young and completely alone, I nonetheless felt peace, tranquility and majesty amidst the cemetery and its surroundings. I found myself insatiably curious of the many different headstones and most especially of the captions I found on them. Though short in length and lacking in content, the captions nevertheless provided a contextual background which allowed me to peer into the life of the deceased. Scarcely able to gauge the significance of these captions, they still captivated my imagination and led to questions of how this person lived his or her life. Was the deceased a person of great importance or fame? Was he or she appreciated and loved by others? Did the deceased positively impact those whom he or she had opportunity to meet? It was always great fun, and often times adventurous, projecting myself into each of these lives, vicariously experiencing the circumstances of my invention. Perhaps the deceased was a scientist whom happened upon significant findings and incredible discoveries. Perhaps he was a great baseball player, a prolific home run hitting third baseman. Maybe an astronaut; that would be exciting! Or, perhaps she was an actress, maybe even a singer or a dancer. My young mind reveled in the seemingly endless possibilities. Yet, in all this joyful dreaming, I eventually woke to the stark reality presented by my surroundings: the deceased, this figment of my youthful imagining, had physically died . . . the grim reaper had come and life had been swallowed up, snuffed out. As I had yet to experience death on a personal level, I was unacquainted with specifically how one might actually physically die. Therefore, the circumstances I equated with causing death were always a bit immature, usually involving horrific accidents via car, train, or plane. I had yet to formulate that the majority of deaths were attributed to more mundane causes such as cancer, heart disease, diabetes, or simply old age. As I would stand by the grave, reflecting on the deceased's manner of death, a truly unsettling notion always entered my mind: my own inevitable date with death would someday come. This alarming thought inevitably caused a cascade of questions: When would I die? How would I die? Would it hurt when I died? I felt so energetic, so full of life that death seemed an utter impossibility and yet I instinctively knew, by proof of the gravesite I had visited, that I, too, would someday die. As I would come to terms with this realization, I inwardly yearned to find answers to the many larger questions surrounding death, questions of a philosophic/religious nature: What happens to the body upon death and burial? Where does our soul go after we die? Do we stay in the grave, awaiting Jesus' return, as I had been taught, or do we immediately go to heaven or hell? The implications of death eluded my young mind; I simply could not make sense of what lay before me.

Despite this time of exhausting reflection, I always ended up feeling grateful for my trip to the cemetery. I felt physically energized, ready to take on my boyhood responsibilities with vigor. As I would leave the cemetery, I knew it would not be long until I would, again, feel the need to reconnect with the dead.

I am now thirty years older and, yet, I ponder death as deeply as when I was a boy. Unlike my childhood, however, I have reached clarity on many of the issues associated with this troublesome subject. Before I expound upon how I reached this clarity, I would like to offer a picture of how I believe the general public currently views death. I have found, amongst American culture, death is viewed as the ultimate adversary, an enemy cloaked in deep and dark secrecy. It is frighteningly enigmatic and a truly bewildering subject, one for whom the average person has little interest in researching. In fact, the majority of the American public is so thoroughly occupied with its daily living; going to work, raising a family, paying the bills, and having fun, that seldom is death given a second thought. Only when death announces its presence, in our lives, does its significance rise up and confront us. In the meantime, we are reminded of death through the lenses of our faith, by what our spiritual authorities teach us. We pray, read our sacred texts, attend church, synagogue, or mosque services and, thus, give notice to death as an intellectual concept. Perhaps we even go so far as to contemplate its spiritual significance on our own eternal existence. Despite this activity, we rarely come to terms with the true personal meaning of death, the true meaning of our physical cessation. We hardly give death more than a fleeting chance of impacting our collective hearts, minds, and souls. We banish the concept to the back of our minds, waiting for another, more convenient time to deal with it. In fact, we become quite adept at avoiding death, even constructing fortresses around our lives to ward off death's inevitability. To keep death at bay, we offer endless prayers for ours and our loved one's personal safekeeping. We plead that neither we, nor those we love, be stricken with disease that would begin the onset of death. We go so far as to offer monetary support to billion dollar corporations, whose only purpose is to help us sustain life and shun death. In spite of this avoidance, we intuitively understand how the unstoppable march of time will bring about our pending date with death, our dreaded nemesis. Yet, in desperate defiance, we disbelieve the facts and keep living as though death will never touch us.

This book, whose subject matter I have contemplated for quite some time, aims to sensibly speak of death and its trappings. Its guiding purpose is to paint a poignant and honest picture of death, while expounding upon death's ramifications for the living. It delves into my many experiences with death, directing funerals, and the particular cases that have impacted me, both positively and negatively. It is therefore written from my professional vantage point, with the overriding goal of educating a vastly misinformed public. To accomplish this goal, I have spent considerable time and money attempting to remedy my own lack of understanding and reach the clarity of which I earlier spoke. I have read countless books, acquired advanced degrees, and have even made my career reflective of this insatiable curiosity of death's mysteries. I presently make my living as a funeral director and, consequently, experience death quite often, through the families I am fortunate to serve. Because of my ongoing acquaintance with death, I feel this work to be inherently authoritative and truly worthwhile; especially to those who may have encountered the sting of death recently. My hope is, after finishing this book; you will have discovered death to be something entirely different from your present imagining. I hope you will have discovered death to be natural, wondrous, and if approached with the correct mindset, a blessing to all affected by its inevitable occurrence. My hope is that you will see your way past the immediate trauma and confusion of death, and accept it not as an ending but a beginning; a rebirth, if you will. And, lastly, my hope is that you will be unafraid to lovingly confront and face death; that you will see it not as the enemy but friend, a most misunderstood companion. As Brad Pitt said, playing the grim reaper in *Meet Joe Black*: "*I can't believe you people. I come for you, and you want to stay. I let you stay and you want to go.*" May we, who await our inevitable calling, simply be those for whom death has no quarrel.

BOOK ONE:

A LIFE TOO SOON TAKEN

CHAPTER 1

THE IMPACT OF A LIFE LIVED WELL

As the bright sun cast its rays through the mortuary's beautiful windows, on a crisp November morning, I recall thinking, "Why in the world am I here? Why am I meeting with this family, who never, in a thousand years, considered this outcome possible?" Feeling a bit agitated, and with no satisfactory reason coming to mind, I quickly shut out the thought; besides, I had business to tend to. Across the desk from me, only a few feet away, sat the husband of the deceased, looking as though he was unaware of his very existence at the moment. I could not help but wonder what this man might be thinking as he gave me a quick glance. Shrunken in his chair, shoulders hunched over, with red, lifeless eyes, he was clothed in a shabby sweat suit that looked as though it was a week or two past its last washing. The scruff on his face seemed about two days old and his overall shabby appearance conveyed his pure indifference of being in my presence. I certainly could not blame him for very few people I know look forward to meeting with me; professionally, that is. My guess was that he would give all that he possessed to be just about anywhere else in the world, save this place. As I began the process of gathering information for a death certificate and obituary notice, it became patently clear this was not going to be an easy process. Death is never easy, of course. For some, it is a bit less invasive and troublesome, as perhaps their loved one's "time to go" was after a long, well-lived existence. For most others, and more specifically, for this young husband, death was a monstrous evil, which had no right to interfere. As I scanned through the information received, a rich tapestry began to form in my mind. The deceased was a young and vivacious woman, who was incredibly devoted to her family, her friends, and her profession. She seemed to be what most people only dreamt of becoming; you know the kind, those few that take hold of life and make it everything they desire. The emerging portrait was that of a person who loved life, every part of life and, as her family continued boasting about her zest for love and life, I could not help but feel a bit envious. Yet, as I glanced back at the husband and could literally feel the pain emanating from his body, I quickly reminded myself of how contented and happy I was.

As the meeting moved along, the family began to open up about the circumstances surrounding their loved one's death. I guessed, by the mere fact that we had yet to receive her body, that she must have been involved in some horrific accident which necessitated her going to the county coroner's office. Unfortunately, I was right. Of all the ways "to go," however, I must admit feeling shocked by hers. You see, she died while riding on, and being thrown from, a very large and powerful bull. I could hardly believe the story as it unfolded. I could have almost understood had there been a terrible car accident or possibly even a motorcycle accident, or a myriad of other "natural" accidental causes of death. Yet, my brain could barely fathom the reasoning behind, what seemed to be, a sheer arbitrary death. "Why did this have to happen," I found myself asking to no one in particular. She had not been that far from the ground; surely, even in a moment of panic, she could have done something to ward off the impact of the trauma. But, alas, it was not to be. Who could understand the reasoning behind this tragedy? I most certainly could not, nor could the traumatized and grieving family, I reckoned.

We finished the preliminaries and, mercifully, our meeting ended for the time being. As I led them to the front door of the mortuary, I nervously stood back a bit, not quite knowing how to send them away. As a funeral director, you are taught never to offer platitudes or religious adages as this would be construed as unprofessional. However, at this most difficult moment, I felt compelled to say something. But what? What could I possibly say that could offer a smidgen of comfort for an utterly comfortless situation? I kept my head down and feebly told them, "I am here for you should you need anything, anything at all." Yet, even with this simple statement, I knew I was lying. Not that what I said was overtly malicious or untrue, of course, but how could I offer them something I did not myself possess? As they turned and walked out the door, I numbly made my way back to the arrangement office. Feeling as though I had just lost a member of my own family, I nevertheless resolved to remain emotionally unattached, for I had work to accomplish, if I were to professionally direct this upcoming funeral.

Despite my resolve, I grappled with this case for quite some time that afternoon and early evening. I had earnest conversations with my colleagues, my wife, and my best friend about this most troubling event and yet, I could not quite make sense of what I was feeling. The most pressing issue, in my opinion, besides the family's suffering, was the spiritual implication of such a tragic death. Was God somehow involved in this dreadful scenario? Would God allow or, even worse, cause this horrific death? I wholeheartedly believed in God; in fact, I had just recently experienced a significantly meaningful spiritual event. My belief, though, offered little hope in resolving this extremely complicated matter. Every inclination of my heart and mind affirmed that this could not possibly be God's work and I felt my soul screaming, "UNFAIR!!" Thus, from a spiritual point of view, this death made absolutely no sense to me. I then thought to myself, "If I am feeling this passionately confused about the deceased's death, what must her loved ones be feeling?" I could not fathom the extreme range of emotions they must have been experiencing.

For the next few days, I did the mundane, but necessary, work of a funeral director. I made all the arrangements with the cemetery, the church, the floral shop, the vault company, the newspaper, etc. I constructed and produced the service folder, moved the deceased into her state room for viewing, and made certain the family was duly informed of all that would be occurring in the days upcoming. This part of the job I could do in my sleep! It is, quite frankly, the rather boring part of a funeral director's existence. Yet, it is the necessary setup for the big event . . . the funeral; the ceremony whereby beleaguered survivors are afforded an opportunity to say goodbye to their loved one. And, in the case of this downtrodden family, I suspected the ceremony would be desperately needed. I surmised that, despite intellectually knowing their goodbyes would go unheeded, saying them would be profoundly meaningful anyway. Such is the significance of the funeral ceremony to grieving families.

Mercifully, the day of the funeral finally arrived. I was feeling a bit on edge, as I anticipated a large crowd to attend this service. Even my boss, the mortuary's owner, would be on hand to assist in the directing of this service. As I entered the church's rather large foyer, I sensed my unease justified for I was immediately confronted by two women who pronounced themselves co-directors of the service. They explained that they were on hand to assure the family's every wish would be heard, adhered to, and acted upon. Frankly, I was not informed of this command structure and I certainly was not expecting it thus I was a little perturbed. Instead of me taking charge, as I have been trained to do, I had to confer with them on everything. This situation made for a very interesting time, to say the least. Nonetheless, I immediately sized up all that had to be accomplished, prior to the service beginning, and the list was daunting. First and foremost, I had to coordinate seating for three very large and diverse groups of people-people who probably had no clue their seats were being reserved. I had to place my staff where I needed them most. I had to keep all the sanctuary doors closed until the musicians finished practicing their songs. I had to find the most logical spot to place the open casket, so as not to offend anyone who did not want to view but also accommodate those who did. I had to ward away well-wishers, so the family might be given opportunity to grieve on their own, prior to the service. And, I had to inform the "co-directors" of all this, prior to doing it! It was one of the most difficult services I have ever had to direct. Yet, in spite of the difficulty, I felt a strong desire to make this as pleasing a service as possible for this devastated family.

The funeral ceremony began on time and proceeded beautifully, without one hiccup. As the fifteen hundred people partook of the service, I could not help but perceive how impacting this young woman's life truly was. By everyone's estimation, she had fully lived her few allotted years on earth. She had given so much of herself to family, friends, acquaintances, organizations, etc., and the stories being told about her selflessness continued unabated for a solid hour. Seemingly, there was no end to the memories created by this beloved woman. By the tone of the stories being shared, this woman's impact would be felt for quite a long time.

After the ceremony concluded, the family and I, along with hundreds of others, made our way to the cemetery to place her body in its final resting place. Being that the cemetery was in the country, far outside of town, we did not go in procession but simply agreed to meet there. I arrived first, so I prepared the casket for the graveside service and subsequent interment. With some assistance, I placed the casket upon the lowering device and awaited the family and friends, who were shortly to arrive.

Standing at the gravesite, with all my work accomplished, I felt a deep sense of serenity move through my body. The sun was beautifully shining, high in the sky, and the country air was clean and crisp. I heard the whisper of a breeze moving through the nearby trees as cattle were bellowing to one another in a field next to me. I was all alone, in utter tranquility. As I stood there, caught up in the emotion of the moment, I again reflected upon the spiritual implications of this young woman's death. This time, however, my mind was not so troubled. I was still unclear as to exactly why her death occurred at this seemingly inopportune time but, after experiencing what I felt at her funeral ceremony and now at the gravesite, I could sense a dramatic change in my feelings. My heart hurt for the family, for their impending and ongoing grief and trial, but, oddly, I felt happy for them as well. This dichotomous feeling shocked me, quite frankly, but I reasoned that the family was able to experience something grand, something more than many of us ever truly experience . . . the wondrous effects of a life majestically lived. To have had someone, so close to them, live an unabashedly outstanding life must have touched them to the very core of their being. They must have felt the very essence of her soul, at times, touching theirs. As a result, their lives must have been positively affected from being so close to her; such was the impact she made on life. I reasoned that perhaps this was the lesson of her early departure and inexplicable death. Maybe this was the deeper spiritual meaning I had intensely struggled to figure out. Perhaps, in the grand scheme of physical life, there are those who come and go quickly, to show us, who are destined to stay longer, how to truly live and truly love. And maybe it is only through this grossly misunderstood concept, death, that the lesson is truly learned by the living.

After the crowd gathered, they prayed fervently, shared moving stories, sang uplifting songs, laughed out loud, and cried un-embarrassingly. They seemed to thoroughly enjoy one another's company. It was as if they had come to celebrate; to send their daughter, wife, mother, sister, aunt, cousin, and friend to her next life. As I stood on the outskirts of the gathering, taking in the scene, I noticed that my own soul had very deeply felt the impact of this moment. As a result, I had decided to live my life, from that moment on, as this woman had: unabashedly, lovingly, and courageously. I doubt that I will ever forget this woman's death; it has made such a mark on my being.

WE WILL NEVER FORGET . . .

We will never forget . . .
The way you loved,
The beauty of your smile,
How you gave of yourself and made life worthwhile.

We will never forget . . .
The way you loved,
The warmth of your touch,
How you softly instructed and taught us so much.

We will never forget . . .
The way you loved,
The melody of your voice,
How you soothed our hearts and helped us rejoice.

We will never forget . . .
The way you loved,
The joy of your essence,
How you changed our lives and made us grateful for your
presence.

Inspiration For
"We Will Never Forget . . ."

What makes someone's life impactful? I have often asked myself this simple question, most often after having taken part in a local celebrity's funeral service. The answer is sometimes elusive as we, the "non-famous," perceive fame to be garnered by accomplishment, wealth, or honor. However, what seems to matter most is simply how the deceased was viewed in their treatment of others. Regardless of how famous someone might have been, their lasting memory always boiled down to their perceived love and appreciation for those around them.

As it regarded this young woman, well known but hardly a celebrity, she was perceived as possessing an immense love for those in her life. As I reflected upon her death and burial, I could not help but think of how impactful her life had truly been. That so many of her friends had come to honor her was a testament to the way she had lived. Yet, what most occupied my thoughts was how she must have affected her family, those whom she interacted with on a continuous basis. What must they have felt, being so closely associated with her?

This poem, then, is what I envisioned her family feeling about the impact of her life upon theirs.

CHAPTER 2

A FAITH NOT EASILY SHAKEN

There are few traumas in life that rival the death of a child. A parent is shaken to the very essence of his or her being when the harrowing news is received. Could there possibly be another scenario which could surpass this moment in its sheer and excruciating pain? I seriously doubt it—and because I have been privy to the agonizing aftermath of such an announcement, and because I have led beleaguered parents through the unbearable process of burial, I can vouch for this firsthand. One specific case stands out, in my mind, as a particularly moving example of this tragic scenario. It involved the death of a young woman who was filled with youthful vitality, exuberance, and joy. She had been preparing herself for life after college, and with a brand new job in her summer plans, she was filled with hope and optimism. However, in a split second, her life was cut short during a horrifying head-on collision on a remote rural highway. Compounding the immense pain and shock of her death, the accident had caused so much damage it rendered viewing of her body nearly impossible. What follows is my account of this case and how the faith of a family; parents, uncles, cousins, etc., moved an entire community to love and peaceful acceptance of an unimaginably tragic death.

When I received notification of this young woman's death, I immediately knew who it was. Through the years, I had come to know her family well, as I had buried many of her relatives. However, unlike this young woman, her family members were well into old age and, though still difficult to endure, death was hardly unexpected in their cases. I felt a bit queasy as I imagined the upcoming meeting, a scenario sure to be filled with tears and a pervasive feeling of sadness. I liken this feeling to the butterflies a live actor must feel, prior to entering the stage of a difficult scene, and, not dissimilar to an actor, the funeral director must maintain his or her professional demeanor, despite the circumstances. In many ways, the director is called to be exactly that: a professional actor; for who would volunteer for such an assignment? Who would want to set across the arrangement table from a mother who has just lost her beloved daughter? Who would voluntarily attempt consoling a father whose heart has been torn asunder by the loss of his only daughter, his baby? Thus, as a funeral director, I am called to act a certain way, regardless of my personal feelings, in order to facilitate the funeral plans being made. Compounding this inherent difficulty, I had an ongoing, established relationship with this family, which only exacerbated the emotional difficulty. There was no buffer zone, so to speak, no place for cool, professional detachment; just a never ending sea of shared grief. As I envisioned the impending encounter, I felt the butterflies turn into a twinge of panic and fear, and immediately begged God for strength to help this family through a terribly painful ordeal.

The moment arrived and, per custom, I greeted the family at the front door of the mortuary. Quite expectedly, I saw the unmistakable signs of grief: red, swollen eyes, looks of confused bewilderment on forlorn faces, and a general lethargy, no doubt attributed to lack of sleep brought on by incessant tears and physical anguish. Immediately, I caught the gaze of the young woman's mother and felt, what seemed to me, a spark of grateful recognition. I could sense relief; that in spite of this excruciating circumstance, my presence would be a comfort for her and her family. We convened in the room nobody wants to find themselves in, the at-need conference room. For many, it is in this room, sitting across from the funeral director, that the awful truth becomes painfully evident. Despite the gloomy circumstances, this room is designed to provide an atmosphere of comfort for the deceased's family members. There is a large and beautiful cherry table, where a good majority of any family can gather and feel themselves part of the proceedings. There are numerous soft and comfortable chairs, a very nice couch, and soft lighting provided by two beautiful table lamps. The room itself is painted in an innocuous, but esthetically pleasing, taupe color. Paintings on the wall depict scenes of utter tranquility and peace; tapestries of floral arrangements and ocean views. The windows are large and casually allow soothing sunlight to caress the room's inhabitants. All in all, if one is forced to be in this room, at the very least, he or she will experience a truly pleasant sensory environment.

As we began the meeting, the family's immense faith and inner strength became quite evident for, rather than waiting on me to direct the proceedings, they jumped right in, offering me encouragement! They insisted that, though their daughter's life was cut short, they were nonetheless thankful, for they wholeheartedly believed she was in a place of unspeakable joy and unimaginable happiness. Now, honestly, I was not in any way expecting this. Utterly dumbfounded, I did not know what to say or how to act. I was certain there would be weeping, even wailing, due to the terrible circumstances of this young woman's death. Yet, this was not the case and I quickly realized I must somehow get hold of my own emotions, lest I be a drain on the family. What an amazing turn of events; quite unlike like any other at-need conference I have experienced. After making the necessary emotional adjustment, I began gathering the preliminary information. While doing this, however, I continually reassessed the family's emotional state and, every so often, noticed signs of sadness; most especially when recounting their loved ones life and looking through photos. I had no doubt as it concerned this family's love for her or of how greatly they would miss her loving presence. However, the way in which they exhibited their unrelenting faith made me step back and quietly reassess my own belief system.

After the arrangements had been made, the inevitable question came: "When can we see her?" Ordinarily, this question would not be an issue as the deceased's body is typically in the mortuary's preparation room, awaiting embalming or whatever may come next, per the service instructions. In a case such as this, however, where traumatic injury has severely disfigured the body, viewing may not be best for anyone. I had already made a phone call to the coroner's office, prior to the family arriving, asking how this young woman appeared; namely, was she viewable? The answer I received was disheartening. The coroner told me in no way would she be viewable as she had sustained traumatic injuries to her head and upper torso and was almost unrecognizable. I surmised that this news would be shocking to the family and, now, I had to tell them. I sat there, like a deer frozen in headlights, unable to formulate the words necessary to convey the dreadful truth. Composing myself, I reluctantly and delicately conveyed this information to the family, who immediately began sobbing. I believe they understood, maybe for the first time, how gruesome an accident this had been and how utterly terrifying it must have been for their little girl at the moment of impact. I braced myself, preparing for the emotional scene I had initially envisioned for this meeting. Yet, no sooner had the crying begun, it ended. I imagine both parents decided to determinedly hold on to hope, however remote it seemed; that they would see and touch their daughter again. Such was the faith they held in their hearts. I instructed them to temper their expectations but added that we would do all we could to make her available to them.

Ordinarily, after this meeting has commenced, the director has a couple of days to complete the necessary arrangements for the upcoming ceremony. However, I was soon to receive a sharply discouraging and rather depressing phone call that would render this timeframe moot. The call came from the coroner's office: they could not positively identify the body and, until they could, she would be kept at their office. As I laid the phone down, I sat in stunned silence. I could not help but think that this family's emotional difficulty and grief had just been multiplied tenfold. Imagine being told your beloved cannot even be physically identified! The pain shot straight to my heart as I personalized this news with visions of my own daughter lying on a cold, metal slab in a cold, emotionless room. Beyond the initial shock of this news, however, I was confronted with the realization that this funeral, which had just been meticulously planned, could not possibly be held on the day the family desired. We would be forced to wait, at least a week, I imagined, as the coroner's office was bringing a dental specialist, from another part of the country, to help with the identification. The responsibility fell on my shoulders to inform the family of this most troubling turn of events. I remember thinking, "What have I done to deserve this trouble?" After this initial bout of self-pity, I realized it was my duty, both as a funeral director and a fellow parent, to inform the family at once. I reasoned that they would prefer hearing it from me, rather than the coroner's office. Yet how does one explain something so horrifying to an already grieving set of parents? I was deeply troubled and, as I sat in the office, internally agonizing over the proper words to convey the un-conveyable, two of the young woman's uncles walked in. They had come to tell me of their assumed role as facilitators between the parents and the mortuary. I was instantly relieved, for their presence as messengers made my job much less burdensome. This is, sad to say, all I was thinking at that particular moment. The uncles sat in stunned silence as I finished explaining this dreadful turn of events. I felt sorry for them both, for the terrible task they now had in front of them.

As the men walked out the door for an undoubtedly distressing meeting with their loved ones, I began to unwind from the day's proceedings. Having accomplished all that I could for the moment, I allowed myself a little respite, to alleviate my frazzled nerves. As I allowed myself to slow down a bit, clarity began to set in, and I conceptualized all that I had just experienced. I compare this time to that brief moment right after a plane lands; you intuitively understand that you are safe but you are still a bit unnerved and shocked at the process. I knew I was far from seeing the other side of these dreadful proceedings and the unknown future haunted me just a bit. How quickly would the coroner's office identify her body? Just how bad would the body look when we received it? Would the parents persist in their desire to see and touch their daughter? These questions were playing tug-o-war with my insides and, try as I might, I could not alleviate the sense of impending dread. I knew that I would have to traverse unknown ground, all the while attempting to shield the parents from awful moments of excruciating pain. But I had no clue as to how I would accomplish this.

I went home, feeling especially grateful to see my wife and two daughters, safe at the dinner table. After spending a somewhat mundane evening at home, complete with a fitful night of sleep, I went back to work the next day feeling emotionally unsettled and physically lethargic. Try as I may, I could not shake the empty feeling I had, not knowing what the future might bring this unfortunate family. I was hoping that all would proceed quickly so the family could get on with their lives and, frankly, so I could get on with mine but, alas, this was not to be. I spent the better part of the next five days going back and forth with the coroner's office and the two uncles. Each time I received new information, I would immediately phone the uncles and let them know the details and they would process the information, then pass it on to the parents. Soon afterward, I would receive a return phone call from the uncles, seeking clarification on an issue or two. Then, they would inevitably ask whether this meant the parents could view their beloved daughter. It became quite exhausting, to say the least; not in the sense that I was being bothered, per se, but simply that I never had good news to share with them. Thus, each time the family would call, I would simply reiterate how sorry I was for their misfortune and restate my vow to work extra hard in making her available to them. I began to lose hope that this case would ever end when, mercifully, the coroner's office called to release the girl's body to us. I was never so relieved! This meant that we could finally proceed with the funeral, albeit cautiously and with deliberate action, due to the condition of the young woman's body and the obvious problem this presented the family.

I was now a step closer to facilitating this funeral but there was one central issue that still needed solving. I had to find a way for the parents to connect with their daughter, via her mangled body, without subjecting them to the shock of her traumatic injuries. Most families use the viewing and/ or visitation time to see, touch and feel their loved one. In this, they receive a sense of closure about their loved one's death. This becomes a tangible representation of their loved one and, although difficult, they are able to process the death much better. Yet, after viewing the young lady myself, I knew there was no way we could present her in any normal fashion as she was just too scarred and broken for this to occur. Then a thought struck me: perhaps they could simply touch and feel part of her body; maybe this would be enough for them to create a sense of meaningful closure. One of the woman's hands had been undamaged and my thought was to keep this hand available to the family, then wrap and clothe the remainder of the body. I called the uncles and presented this scenario to them but they offered me little consolation, as they had no idea how their loved ones would react to this idea. I hung up the phone and remember feeling a deep sense of desperation for the family, for I knew they were suffering terribly over this perplexing obstacle. In what seemed like seconds, however, the family called right back and told me this scenario was acceptable to them; that they would be happy with simply having her hand available to touch. They were also bringing her favorite college sweat suit, for the mortuary to clothe her in. I was again truly relieved and ever grateful for their understanding, as this arrangement was absolutely the best possible scenario for all involved; the family, the public, and the mortuary.

After finally dressing and casketing the young woman, the moment arrived for her family to view. I had prepared them for what they were about to see, as even with the wrapping of her body, there was still the inherent problem of what to do with her head and face. My colleagues and I decided to wrap them in surgical gauze, out of necessity, but this made her look too much like a mummy. We then decided to place a scarf over her head and face and use the hood of the sweatshirt to cover her head. I was a bit apprehensive about this entire "display," but concluded there was literally nothing else we could do, other than having a closed casket (which, according to the family, was out of the question). As they entered the mortuary, the family looked much different from when I saw them last. Being that it was literally a week after the initial at-need meeting, they had an entirely different and peaceful look about them. No longer were their eyes red, nor their countenance depressed; conversely, I felt a spark of joy emanating from them. They seemed to be at peace with all that had transpired and I recall thinking how admirable that was. I stepped forward, took the mother by the hand, and led her into the viewing room. With the rest of the family following, I showed the mother and the father their beloved daughter and then quietly exited the room. As I walked out of the room, and into the hallway, I said a quiet but passionate prayer that God would grant this family the courage and consolation they needed to endure this most difficult time. My prayer was answered, for when they came out of the viewing room, they told me how immensely grateful they were for how we presented her. She looked fabulous, they said, and they were absolutely thankful for our efforts.

That night, as I left the mortuary for home, I could not help but to deeply contemplate all that I had experienced with this family. I had to admit that I was not in the same place, spiritually speaking, as they were. They seemed to have such a deeply abiding faith; a faith which truly brought them comfort in what seemed, to me, an utterly comfortless situation. I was quite perplexed as rarely have I experienced this set of circumstances while working at the mortuary. In fact, most often, I experience the exact opposite, whereby parents are barely consolable and wanting nothing more than the moment to mercifully end. Yet, this family seemed impervious to the happenings and comforted one another with a deep and abundant love. Later in the evening; after dinner was eaten, the kid's homework completed, and T.V. watched, I spoke with my wife about the day's happenings. She agreed with me, about what an extraordinary circumstance I found myself in. She thought it a little strange but, inspiring nonetheless, how this family had reacted to such a tragic event. We discussed the cause of their remarkable acceptance and wondered if, perhaps, we would emulate this had we found ourselves in this situation. Unable to reach conclusion, we simply hoped we would arise to this level of understanding if, God forbid, we ever found ourselves facing this tragedy. I, however, promised myself a more in-depth consideration, a deeper examination of my heart and soul, after all the proceedings had taken place.

The following morning arrived, the day of the young woman's funeral. It was being held in a medium-sized church and, due to the expected crowd, they decided to broadcast the service into the church gymnasium. As an experienced funeral director, I have taken part in some rather large, unconventional, and extremely out-of-the ordinary funeral services. I have been involved in services where the FBI has assisted for fear of public retaliation on the family we were serving. I have even been involved in a service where there was a bomb threat. Nothing like that was expected at this young woman's service, of course, but I knew we would have standing-room-only seating and, because the church had precious little space to begin with, I had to take charge or it could become a fiasco. Thus I went about my business of directing; putting the staff in the places I wanted them, giving them specific direction as to what their responsibilities were, and, finally, tending to the family's needs. Thankfully, all proceeded according to plan, with both the church and the gymnasium filled to the brim, and finally the moment arrived for the service to begin. I was at the head of the casket and one of my colleagues was at the foot. Just prior to processing in, however, the mother of the deceased placed a tiny white linen dress on top of the casket. Apparently, this was the dress her young daughter wore while being baptized and the shock of this moment immediately affected all who were nearby. I cannot begin to express how immensely difficult this was; how hard it was for all to continue. To witness such an excruciatingly emotional moment, while trying to maintain my professional demeanor, was simply impossible. I immediately began tearing up, all the while trying desperately to think of anything that would take my mind off this scene. To this day, I shed a tear, thinking of how precious and amazingly meaningful this moment was, and how fortunate I was to take part.

I recall very little of the rest of the service as it was simply a blur. Afterwards, the procession to the cemetery was at least a mile long and, upon arrival, it took us the better part of twenty minutes just to gather all the people at the graveside. Most of those gathered would not be able to hear the minister recite the final commendation yet I hardly think this mattered. They simply were there out of respect, love, and admiration for the family. I remember thinking, upon leaving the cemetery, that I had just witnessed something profound. I had taken part in an event of monumental importance; an event of timeless impact for my soul, as this young woman was deeply loved and immensely cherished by so many. I concluded that her death would leave an indelible mark on me as well as the multitude of people who had come that day. We had simply witnessed love and faith being expressed in its fullest depths and, regardless of whether we wanted to acknowledge it or not, death had brought this all about. Though most would argue death was too quick in taking this young soul, none would argue the impact it brought upon us all.

The Face Of Love Encountered

Never did I see, nor did I hear.
A face so lovely, a voice so dear.

Unbeknownst to my cognition, I have passed
beyond this field of vision.
To a place most wonderful to see; could this
indeed, be eternity?

As I feel myself moving farther and farther,
the light up ahead is growing larger and larger.
As the light is appearing brighter and brighter,
my body begins feeling lighter and lighter.

Inexplicable, is this feeling I'm experiencing.
So utterly happy, I feel like I am dancing.
Into this light whose warmth is inviting, I no
longer feel the need of fighting.

I place myself fully into the lap of love, who
presence I can only assume is from above.
My friends, my loved ones, they are all here.
They greet me with a hearty and loving cheer.

Who is it that now appears, in my vision; oh so
clear?
The face I glimpsed upon my death, whilst I
took my final breath?
Yes, it is him, it is her; it is the one I know for
sure . . . the face of love alone, the face I have
always, always known.

Inspiration For "The Face Of Love Encountered"

As I prepared for this family's visit, to put together funeral arrangements, I momentarily placed myself in the young woman's shoes, at the moment of her crash. I tried to imagine what she must have thought and felt during this horrific accident.

Being one who wholeheartedly believes in life after death, I felt God would be in the midst of this young woman's vision, upon her horrifying physical death. In my own mind, due to the nature of her death, I felt her soul would need consoling; that in a sense, she would require quick clarification of what had just occurred. More than anything, I felt she would need to be surrounded by pure love, to help guide her soul where it was intended to go. Thus, I felt her loved ones who had gone before, would be on hand, to assist in her transition to Paradise.

This poem, then, reflects my own thought process, as it pertains to how this young woman would have experienced her final few moments on Earth and her transition into the presence of God.

CHAPTER 3

THE VISIT I LOATHED TO TAKE

Have you ever had one of those days where you wished you could have simply stayed in bed, called in sick, and played hooky all day? Well, let me tell you my story of one of those days.

The day began as any other: I awoke, got myself and the girls out of bed, had some breakfast, and, after dropping the girls off at school, went to work. It was a spring day, majestically beautiful as I recall, with the sun glaringly bright in the Eastern sky and just a hint of a soothing breeze in the air. It was the perfect day for golf, which, not so coincidentally, was my true aspiration for the day. In spite of this desire, I trudged into work anyway. As a funeral professional, the one thing you can count on is surprise, as death adheres to no schedule. Thus, after arrival at work, and the downing of a few cups of coffee, I received a phone call announcing a pending death. Ordinarily, this type of call is made by the family of an older person. This family typically wants to set an appointment to pre-arrange a funeral service, so they do not have to make decisions all at once. However, to my chagrin, this call was something altogether different, made on behalf of a little girl, not quite thirteen years old, who had cancer. I was a little jolted as I talked with the father of the sick girl. Being that my oldest daughter had just recently turned eleven, this was a little too close for comfort. Compounding the difficulty was the fact that the family, primarily the mother, wanted me to come to the hospital where their little girl was being treated. She wanted me to meet her sick daughter, and the rest of the family, prior to making arrangements with our funeral home. As I understood it, they essentially wanted to interview me, and the mortuary, to see if we were a good fit for their family. I was a bit taken aback as I had never fielded this sort of request, prior to this day. I agreed to the arrangement but, as I hung up the phone, I immediately began feeling a little nervous. It was a little like the feeling one has when interviewing for a deeply desired job; sweaty palms, racing heart, uncontrollable nervousness. I began anticipating all the questions that might be asked of me, questions like: Have you worked with children before? Do you have children of your own? Do you have nice caskets for kids? What do you charge for children's funerals? To be honest, I was hesitant to make this trip for, as a funeral director, I am vastly familiar with the post-death protocol, but hardly before. Occasionally, families bring in their loved one, prior to death, to speak of pre-arrangement options but this is rare. More common is the meeting after death has occurred; thus, to meet the person for whom these arrangements were being made, a child no less, was immensely troublesome.

Nevertheless, I packed a few items I intended to give the parents, and headed for the hospital. On the way, my mind wandered a bit, as I was thinking of how to make the best impression. Would I try to be funny? Would I be dour and "professional?" Would I try to engage the little girl in conversation, if this were even possible? What was expected of me to make this appointment a success? I had hardly a clue; all I knew is that I needed to project warmth and understanding to both this young girl and her family. Perhaps this was all they needed to make their decision. The girl was in the children's intensive care unit, awaiting death's call, as there was nothing more the doctors could do for her. I understood, from the initial phone call, that she had struggled with cancer since age three. It had been more than three years since her last bout with the dreaded disease but this time the doctors held little hope for recovery, as the cancer had metastasized and spread throughout the little girl's body. She had precious little time left and, as I entered the hospital and made my way to the children's floor, the butterflies kept flittering around in my stomach. I cannot begin to convey the sense of dread and utter helplessness I felt prior to this encounter. Nobody prepares for this type of meeting; indeed, how can one anticipate a scenario such as this in the first place?

I entered the elevator and pushed the button corresponding to the floor where the family was gathered. I said a short, internal prayer, asking for peace and comfort, for myself and for this unfortunate family. As I exited the elevator, and headed for the nurse's station, I was immediately recognized by one of the ICU nurses; I guess it was the suit I had on (always a give-away for a funeral professional), and suddenly found myself surrounded by three of these ladies. They wanted to "prep" me for my meeting with the family. They had come to know this family very well and wanted to convey how much they cared for this little girl and her parents. They told me she was so sweet and loving and that it broke their collective hearts to see her in this condition. She was a model patient; never complaining, always smiling and ever respectful, saying yes ma'am or no ma'am. She intuitively knew what was occurring and yet, she carried herself with such amazing dignity, you would have believed her to be much older than her twelve years. The parents were special as well as they were devoted to their little girl, spending countless hours, day and night, at the hospital. The parents were constantly encouraging the staff; bringing treats and cards for everyone, remembering birthdays, special occasions and the like. The nurses could hardly contain their emotion as they recounted these facts. Thus, prior to even meeting the little girl and her parents, I had a healthy dose of emotion heaped upon me.

After gaining their composure, the nurses took me to the waiting area where the family had gathered. As I stepped into the room, which was noticeably full, I had trouble spotting exactly who the parents were, in and amongst all the people. Not wanting to be ignorantly presumptuous, I waited a bit for the parents to step forward and greet me. As I waited, however, there was a rather awkward silence as everyone directed their attention toward me but nobody spoke. The air in the room seemed incredibly stuffy; I could hardly breathe as I awaited the introductions. After what seemed like an eternity, I finally just blurted out, "Hi, I'm Colin." From the corner of the room, a lady came forward and introduced herself as Linda, the young girl's mother. She was elegantly dressed, in a light brown pant-suit, with a pressed white cotton top and nice black shoes. She had an authoritative presence, something I could sense as I walked forward to greet her. I surmised that she possessed a quiet courage and steely determination, which was used to steer herself, her family, and her daughter through these extremely trying times. I assumed she would be my primary contact, even as her husband stepped forward, albeit slightly behind her. She greeted me with a somewhat indifferent handshake, no doubt hesitant to make my acquaintance, and began introducing me to everyone in the room. It was a surreal experience, as everyone knew my purpose for being there and treated me accordingly. Hesitantly, she began recounting the history of her daughter's sickness; how she and her husband quickly noticed something wrong while the little girl was a toddler. She recalled, with tears welling in her eyes, the day they learned of the cancer diagnosis and how difficult the intervening years of remission and advance had been on everyone. Yet, her family had resolved to beat this dreadful disease; to find the specialists necessary to help the little girl through her troubles. They vowed to keep a positive frame of mind and to support their little girl the best they knew how. She recounted the numerous trips they had taken, around the country, meeting with specialist after specialist. They would receive hope for a while but then have it crushed in another round of cancer's devastating advance. In a desperate and final move, they checked the girl into the Mayo clinic, hoping for a miraculous and new intervention, something that would offer a determinate hope for the future. It was after this final round of medical treatment that they believed the cancer to be gone; that their little girl was truly healed of the life-consuming cancer cells. Thus, when they received news of this final, shocking advancement of the hideous cancer, they were utterly devastated and knew the end to be near. When she finished her disheartening story, I simply wanted to hug her as I felt so sad. I must not have concealed my feelings all that well for Linda quickly stepped forward and touched my hand, offering me consolation, as my eyes filled up with tears. Though my intention had been to project warmth and understanding, I nonetheless felt I was failing miserably as a funeral director. I needed to get hold of myself and become a source of strength and guidance for this family's impending hardship.

Somebody, from across the room, said something funny and the entire collection of people suddenly burst into laughter. I was so relieved! I do not know what I would have done had this tension-filled moment not abated. Linda then sauntered out of the room and motioned for her husband, and me, to follow. As we walked down the hallway, en route to her daughter's room, she began telling me about her daughter's present condition. Though nearing the end, her little girl was still fairly cognizant and aware of her surroundings. Thus, Linda made it clear that I was to remain positive, treating her daughter as I would any other twelve year-old. I assured her I would do just as she asked as we walked into the little girl's room. The room was adorned in a very colorful, Disney-like motif, with large paintings of cute animals, balloons, and rainbows. Despite the dreary circumstance, the room was pleasing to the eye and brought a bit of comfort in an otherwise comfortless situation. Miley, the cancer-stricken young girl, was sleeping at the moment and neither Linda nor her husband saw the need to wake her. Thus, we just stood there, lovingly looking over the little girl's dilapidated and depleted body, whilst she peacefully slept. Had I not known better, I would have mistakenly assumed the girl to be suffering from the flu or some other non-life threatening malady. Yet, here she was, barely holding onto life while cancer wreaked havoc on her insides. Linda commented on how courageous Miley had been whilst fighting this unrelenting enemy; how she had not given into depression or sadness and how she looked forward to meeting her deceased grandfather in heaven. It was almost more than I could bear. I simply could not understand how Miley could face such a terrible ordeal with such calm dignity, and at such a young age. More than that, I could hardly fathom how strong her parents were in facing these dreadfully agonizing circumstances. To know that a part of your very self is being taken from you, while being utterly powerless to affect the outcome, must be excruciatingly painful to endure. As if sensing my heartache, Linda and her husband made a motion for us to exit the room. The three of us then found a quiet place to discuss the particulars of how our mortuary could best serve their family.

I do not remember all the particulars of this meeting nor does it make any difference, I suppose. The bottom line was that both Linda and her husband felt a connection with me that day; enough to trust me with their most precious little girl and her funeral arrangements. It was not quite two weeks after this meeting that little Miley succumbed to her cancer and I received the disheartening call from Linda. She phoned me on my cell and calmly related the dreadful news to me. However, she seemed completely different than I would have expected her, given what had just occurred. As if right on cue, she related that although Miley's death was more than she, or her husband, could bear, their faith in God would see them through. She stated that Miley had suffered much through her few allotted years on Earth and that, now, she was no longer in pain but in the presence of unbelievable love and peaceful serenity. For this she was utterly ecstatic. I told her that I believed this very same thing and that I looked forward to helping her and her family celebrate Miley's life in a way that was befitting of the little girl's courage and strength. We made the at-need appointment for the next morning.

The funeral was lovely; the plans proceeded exactly as they were drawn up. The service was heavily attended and, amidst the air of sadness, an abiding and abounding joy was experienced as well. All who attended surely recognized the quiet dignity, love, and courage of this little family; a family who had just lost part of its collective heart to cancer. Yet, through it all, they remained faithful and encouraging to one another and to all who happened to step into their lives. As I left the cemetery, following the young girl's burial, I was once again moved by what I had experienced through Miley's death. Even at such a young age, Miley had taught so much to so many. She showed all how to possess and express dignity, strength, love, courage, and faith—in the midst of painful uncertainty. In the years since Miley's death, I have often recalled what I learned from her. Whenever life becomes burdensome, I remember Miley and put into practice what she, through her death, taught me. I feel so incredibly fortunate.

As I Lie Here

As I lie here, feigning sleep, trying desperately my courage to keep; I think of my mother and my father.

They truly love me, this I know, taking care of me as I grow; but I want not to be a bother.

In this room of many colors, I suddenly feel the presence of others; speaking of me in a guarded tone.

Though I'm cared for in every way, I am looking forward to the day; when I will no longer be alone.

For, in just a little while I will fly away with a smile; to the home for which I was destined.

To see my Father who awaits me, saying goodbye to my loving family; knowing the burden has been lessened.

Though I love them oh so much, often longing for their touch; I know they have suffered greatly.

So, for now, I say goodbye, and though I know they will cry; we will soon meet again in that mansion so stately!

Inspiration For "As I Lie Here"

As I stood beside the bed of the cancer-stricken little girl, talking with her parents, I could not help but think she knew we were there. And, in that precise moment, I felt an immensity of love welling up, from deep inside, desiring to take all her pain away.

Obviously, there was nothing I, nor her parents, could do but, as I left the hospital that day, I deeply pondered what she must have been thinking during this brief encounter. This poem is the fruit of my imagining.

A Collection
Of Associated
Poetry

AT THE GRAVESIDE

Standing at the graveside, a gentle breeze caresses my face.
As the sun peaks through the clouds, I prepare myself for the final goodbye.

The casket sits atop the apparatus, as if suspended in mid-air.
The flowers; beautiful in pinks and reds, adorn the site.

Friends and loved ones, they have all gathered 'round.
To support me in this final gesture of life's finality.

Who could have known death's calling would have been so quick?
Who could have foreseen life being taken so soon?

But, alas, death cannot be questioned.
It has the final say and offers no explanations.

So, I must move on, complete my own life's journey.
Without the love I leave behind at the graveside this day.

Inspiration For "At The Graveside"

One day, while I was preparing for a graveside funeral service, I had everything accomplished and was simply waiting for the family and minister to arrive so we could begin the service. As I waited, the sun kept poking in and out of the partly cloudy skies above and a gentle, soothing breeze blew on my face. As I looked at the grave site, I noticed the casket, sitting atop the lowering apparatus, and it looked as though it was suspended in mid-air. I had never given notice to this before and was quite mesmerized with it.

As the family and friends began arriving, I pondered how the daughter of the deceased must be feeling, saying good bye to her mother. The deceased was very old but still truly loved by many and even though her time on Earth was long, her death had occurred rather abruptly. Thus, the daughter was fairly emotional as she said goodbye that day. I felt empathy for her and hoped that she would recover her joy soon.

This poem was a simple reflection of this moment in time and my response to the profound and moving circumstances surrounding the burial of a loved one.

I WANT NOTHING OF YOU

Death . . .

Who can understand your purpose?
Who can understand your process?
Who can understand your timing?

Mere mortals, we are, tarrying in angst while we await
your approach.
We see you from afar, we feel you in our bones.

Yet, continually living, we blissfully ignore your call.
We experience the joys of our own heartbeat,
                    the sounds of our own breathing,
                    the creation of our own hands.

In all this, we shun your presence, only occasionally
heeding your signals.

For only when the march of time comes calling will
you be forced upon us and we will scream . . .

"Depart from me, for I want nothing of you."

Inspiration For
"I Want Nothing Of You"

In preparation for the book, "Up Close & Personal: Stories of Courage in the Midst of Devastation," I felt the need to write an organized introduction. This introduction was a means of explaining why I would undertake such a work in the first place. As I put pen to paper, I wanted to convey how much American culture utterly loathes the concept of death; how it shuns the idea until confronted with its reality.

This poem is a response to this idea of shunning death, of ignoring its lifelong call, all the while knowing it is there. It is this idea of putting death away, until it grabs out attention, which fascinates me, especially in the profession I find myself part of.

THE GREAT BEYOND

I sit here today, wasting away; with cancer taking its
best shot.
I have little doubt that my heart will give out; despite
fighting with all I have got.

Friends convey to me their heartfelt sympathy; for the
predicament I find myself in.
Yet there is something I feel, so amazingly real; now,
let me clue you in.

So often at night, when I am full of fright; about my
future unknown.
A presence comes to me, too blessed to explain you
see; yet thrilling down deep in my bones.

A feeling so warm, so bright, it fills me with delight;
causing me to question no more.
Though my body gives out, my soul is preparing to
shout; for the day I arrive on that shore.

Thus, death beckons me to follow, leaving this body so
hollow; for the place my soul is drawn.
Though I know not what awaits, I eagerly anticipate my
date; my moment in the great beyond.

INSPIRATION FOR "THE GREAT BEYOND"

Every now and then, in the funeral business, you meet a person for whom you feel an immediate connection. This person might be someone entirely different than you but you feel as though you have known them a lifetime. Often times, this connection is made with someone for whom death is imminent.

This poem was written in response to just such a person. I have been visiting for a little under two years, as of this writing, with this gentleman and his wife. They, along with their very friendly dog, have become dear friends of mine. In my visits with them, we often talk deeply on the subject of death and what awaits this gentleman as his death approaches. These times become quite extraordinary in scope and are in no way common to my every day experiences as a funeral director.

Though death is in his immediate future, my friend is unafraid and prepared to confront this reality. His wife shares these views and thus is prepared as well. When the moment arises, I know they will view it as a beginning of something glorious and grand, not an ending. My friend, I know, will then experience the beauty and majesty of the Great Beyond.

THE BEAUTY OF DEATH
AFTER LIFE

Into this world of struggle was I born, on one eerily
desperate morn.
Invited not of my own volition, to a circumstance not of
my own intention.
Cast into an existence I never selected; thrust into a life I
never expected.

Such were the circumstances of my birth.

Living a life of meager existence; eking out a living
with little assistance.
Watching the world as it passes me by, with nary a concern
for me in its eye.
Wondering why I was born in the first place; never
knowing the beauty of my own face.

Such are the circumstances of my life.

I see, at long last, a cure, a remedy, for my decidedly
difficult life of misery.
I envision beauty not-transcended; a glory awaits me after
this life has ended.
An existence full of unending bliss, complete with the
softness of God's sweet kiss.

Such will be the circumstances of my death.

Inspiration For "The Beauty Of Death After Life"

One day, while watching the world news, I was struck by the brutality of life in a war-torn country. It got me to thinking of what it must be like to be born amongst such unabated death and devastation. What could life offer to someone who only experiences hatred, anger, frustration and hopelessness? Quite possibly, someone in this position would view death as beautiful, for in death, they would escape the madness of life.

Through this poem, there is the veiled thread of the subject of suicide. Though I don't advocate suicide, I feel that I understand, somewhat, why someone would consider it as an option. Having experienced the difficulty of death by suicide, as a funeral director, I can only say that those left in its wake find it extraordinarily burdensome to deal with.

On the surface, then, the title of this poem makes little sense. For what beauty can be found in death? Ordinarily, we think of death as tragic, as an ending to the beauty of life. Yet, what if this life was tragic, in and of itself? What if one's expectations, after death, are much better than the reality being experienced in life? This is, ultimately, what this poem was meant to convey.

OH DADDY:
A YOUNG GIRL'S LAMENT

Oh, daddy, you left me so quickly,
I never thought I'd see you this way.
You had never been one to be sickly,
Yet now I say bye to you today.

In the casket I see your lifeless face,
Though your essence I do not recognize.
Your presence in my mind I can never erase,
Especially your loving and joy-filled eyes.

Why you had to go I'll never understand,
I wanted you to always be in my life.
To be the one who would give my hand,
To the boy who asked me as his wife.

To see my children grow and to learn,
This was my joy, my expectation.
Involved in their lives, each in their turn,
Offering them love, with no hesitation.

But now this dream is no longer here,
I know that I must move on.
You have left me but I know you're near,
For to your presence is my heart drawn.

So, daddy, I do not blame you for leaving,
Because I know it wasn't your choosing.
To God you must be now cleaving,
But God, understand it is me that is losing.

Inspiration For
"Oh Daddy:
A Young Girl's Lament"

Sometimes, in my profession, a death occurs which causes even the hardest of individuals emotional difficulty. This death usually involves someone "young," who seemingly has much of life still to live. It is so shocking and utterly befuddling that it catches the public by surprise and, very often, elicits an incredible response.

This poem is in response to such a death. The individual was a man in his early 40's, outwardly healthy looking, who exhibited no signs of health problems. He had a wife and two children; a 19 year-old son and a 13 year-old daughter. My interpretation of what this young girl must have been feeling and thinking, upon discovering her father dead, is the subject matter of this poem.

As I also have a young daughter this age, I could almost feel the pain of this young girl. I must admit that I am typically a cry-baby, when it comes to things of the heart so this funeral was especially difficult for me. This poem, then, was an outlet for my emotion, a way to process this death in a meaningful way.

THE RAIN FALLS SOFT

The rain falls soft today and it's echoing how I feel.
My best friend went away; I can't believe this is real.

The rain falls soft today and it's landing on her grave.
Her body rests in the clay; though she was oh so brave.

The rain falls soft today and it's running down my
cheek.
Death is lonely and gray, making me empty and weak.

The rain falls soft today and it's collecting on the
ground.
Washing the sorrow my way; despite its soothing
sound.

The rain falls soft today and it's seeping through my
clothes.
Death has denied her stay; making me miserable and
morose.

The rain falls soft today and it's comforting to my
touch.
She has been swept away; I still miss her so very
much.

The rain falls soft today and it's soaking me to the
bone.
Without her in my life to stay; I feel so much alone.

The rain falls soft today and I must somehow get dry.
My heart is still broken I say; but I know she'd want me to try.

The rain falls soft today and it's delicate as a flower.
Though I leave you this way; my love, I'll see you with the
coming shower.

INSPIRATION FOR
"THE RAIN FALLS SOFT"

I had a funeral where a man buried the love of his life, his wife of 63 years. He was obviously old and gray; yet he was still in possession of all his faculties. He knew exactly how he wanted to the service to go and I set about doing all that he wished.

The service, I recall, was nice, as services go. Even with the woman dying at an advanced age, the service was well attended. As we got to the gravesite, rain began to fall. It was the kind of rain that wasn't necessarily a nuisance but more a gentle soaking. I remember thinking that perhaps, metaphorically, God was crying, noticing how grief stricken the husband was. It was an interesting thought.

The graveside committal service finished and as the people began to leave, I noticed the gentleman step aside, away from others, and begin whispering to the casket. From a distance, I obviously could not hear what he was uttering, but I could feel his sadness at that moment. It is something I'll never quite forget.

This poem is a reflection of how I imagined him to have felt during this moment.